ffro the sentence of this tretys lyte
After the Which this murye tale I Wryte
And ther fore herkneth What pt I schal seye
And lat me tellen al my tale I preye

℩Explicit⹂

℩Heere bigynneth Chaucers tale of me libe

[...]oung man called melibeus myght
[...]p on his Wyf that called Was Pr
[...]ughter that called Was Sophie·[...]
[...] for his desport is Went in to the f
his Wyf and eek his doghter· hath he left With h[...]
the dores Cheren faste yschett ℩The of hise olde foo
And setten laddres to the Walles of his hous and
ben entred And betten his Wyf and Woundes h[...]
fyue mortal Woundes in fyue sondry places Thi[...]
hir feet· in hir handes· in hir eyys· in hir nose·
And leften hir for deed And Wenten aWey ℩W[...]
torned Was in to his hous and saugh al this m[...]
Was man rentynge his clothes gan to Weye an[...]
ce his Wyf as ferforth as she dorste bisoghte hym
ffor to styute but nat for thy he gan to crie and
the moore ℩This noble Wyf Prudence remembres
sentence of Ouide in his book that cleped is the re[...]
Wep as he seith he is a fool that destourbeth the mo[...]
the deeth of hys child til she haue Wept hir fille a[...]
tyme ℩And thanne shal man doon his diligence
Wordes hir to reconforte and preyen hir of hir W[...]
styute ℩ffor Which reson this noble Wyf prudence
housbonde for to Wepe and crie as for a certein sp[...]
she caughte hir tyme she seyde hym in this Wise [...]
lord quod she Why make ye youre self for to be [...]
this it apyteneth nat to a Wys man to maken Wic[...]

Geoffrey Chaucer

SCALA

Michael Alexander

Geoffrey Chaucer's most famous work is his *Canterbury Tales*, a set of tales told by pilgrims on their way to the shrine of St Thomas Becket at Canterbury Cathedral. The pilgrimage was very popular, so popular indeed that the kind of tall tales told by travellers became known as 'Canterbury tales'. Chaucer opens the Prologue to his work with pilgrims assembling in a tavern to set off for Canterbury from London. Next morning, the morning of 18 April, the pilgrims ride out. Chaucer later gives us astronomical indications that tell us the year is 1387. He is the best-known poet in English before William Shakespeare, and as good a writer as any after Shakespeare. Chaucer's name occurs 400 times in public records, but as a royal servant, not as a poet.

FRONTISPIECE: *Miniature portrait of Chaucer in the margin of the Ellesmere Manuscript of c.1410, the most handsome of the eighty-six manuscripts of the* Canterbury Tales. *Chaucer points to the* Tale of Melibee, *which he is about to tell. The face is fine, the legs too short, as the figure has been adapted from a non-equestrian archetype.*

RIGHT: *Miniature portrait of the Squire in the Ellesmere Manuscript of the Tales, c.1410, in the margin opposite the tale he is to tell. The youthful Squire is an apprentice Knight, very fashionably dressed, on a prancing horse. In his teens, Chaucer had himself served in battle in France.*

OPPOSITE: *Chaucer reciting his* Troilus and Criseyde *to the Court. This famous painting is the frontispiece to a manuscript of the* Troilus. *In an idealised scene, a younger Chaucer stands in a pulpit surrounded by the 'younge, fresshe folkes, he or she' to whom his great poem is addressed. The manuscript was probably commissioned by Charles d'Orleans (see p.24).*

EDWARDVS   III

Chaucer's Times

The late fourteenth century was often turbulent. When Chaucer was born, probably in 1342, England's prestige was at its height: King Edward III and his son the Black Prince had been victorious in Scotland and were about to win great victories in France, beginning the Hundred Years War. The bubonic plague known as the Black Death arrived in England in 1348, eventually killing one-third of its people. When the plague had passed, many serfs left the fields they had worked for the Lord of the Manor, and walked to market to sell their labour. Bonded labourers became free men; the economy became more cash-based and mercantile, less service-based and feudal.

When the old King died in 1377, he was succeeded by his grandson Richard, the only surviving son of the Black Prince. Richard II was aged ten. In 1381 he had to face the Peasants' Revolt in which the London palace of his uncle John of Gaunt was sacked, and Archbishop Sudbury murdered in the street. In 1386 Richard lost his power, and Chaucer also lost his official posts. Richard regained power in 1389, but was deposed ten years later by Henry IV. The Church too had its troubles. John Wyclif, an Oxford theologian, had been criticising clerical abuses and questioning some teachings. In 1387 the rival claimants to the Papacy, in Avignon and Rome, divided the loyalties of western Christians.

OPPOSITE: *Edward III, King of England, 1327–77, painted by an unknown artist, oil on panel, 1590–1610. Edward restored England's military prestige, reversing his father's defeats in Scotland and winning major victories in France early in the Hundred Years War, helped by his eldest son the Black Prince.*

LEFT: *Historiated initial 'C' of* Clerici, *clerics, from* Omne Bonum, *1360–75, an alphabetically arranged encyclopaedia. Young monks with plague-spotted faces are shown being blessed by an abbot or bishop. The Black Death killed about one-third of the people of England when Chaucer was about seven years old.*

Numquid adheret tibi sedes iniqui
tatis: qui fingis laborem in precepto.
Captabunt in animam iusti: et san
guinem innocentem condempnabūt.

The troubles of his times scarcely appear in Chaucer's voluminous writings. The Black Death is the backdrop to his Pardoner's Tale; and a mention of 'the cherles rebellynge' is one of Chaucer's two allusions to the Peasants' Revolt. Other social ills of Chaucer's day are quite prominent in the *Tales*; he observed the antics of human beings with a satirical humour.

The *Tales* follow a tradition of satirical writing known as estates satire, focusing on sharp practice in the professions, in finance and commerce, and in some of the clergy. Chaucer's method is not the moral denunciation usual in estates satire, but ironical praise. He speaks admiringly of the Monk's splendid attire and of the Prioress's fashionable manners and love for her little dogs. His writing has a quick, unsettled tone,

which may reflect the uncertainty and instability of the world he lived in. He also has a wide, shrewd and (mostly) benign understanding of human nature.

ABOVE: *Men ploughing with a team of oxen. Most Englishmen lived by working the land. Chaucer shows the Ploughman as one of the few pilgrims who is wholly good. From the Luttrell Psalter, c.1325–35.*

OPPOSITE: *This panel of Richard II, aged about thirty, is the first-known contemporary painted portrait of an English sovereign.*

PAGES 10–11: *An illustration to the Chronicle of Jean Froissart (before 1483), a French contemporary of Chaucer. It shows Wat Tyler, a leader of the Peasants' Revolt in 1381, about to be killed by William Walworth, Mayor of London, at the parley in Smithfield with Richard II, aged fourteen. On the right, Richard addresses his troops.*

RIGHT: *April (here 'Apriell') from stained glass depicting the Labours of the Months at the Church of St Mary and All Saints, Checkley, c.1535–45. The activity of this spring month is to go out into the fields. The young man holds up both the flower and the 'tendre croppes' mentioned by Chaucer in his April opening to the Pilgrimage.*

The Tales

Chaucer's famous Prologue to his collection of tales recounts how he joins a group of pilgrims assembling in Southwark to ride to the shrine of St Thomas Becket at Canterbury Cathedral. It is April. His twenty-nine pilgrims are at the Tabard Inn in Southwark, the suburb linked to the City by London Bridge. Chaucer joins his fictional pilgrims and becomes a character in his own story: 'So hadde I spoken with hem everichon / That I was of hir felaweshipe anon.' (I had spoken to each of them in such a way that soon I was one of their company.) The Host, or landlord, of the Tabard proposes to the pilgrims that, as they ride to Canterbury, they should pass the time in a tale-telling game. The jovial Host is to be referee and judge, and the pilgrims are to return to his inn at the end of their pilgrimage, to stay and enjoy a dinner, which will cost the teller of the best tale nothing. The pilgrims agree to this proposition, the commercial basis of which will not have escaped Chaucer, a Collector of Customs.

In spring, Chaucer begins, people love to visit foreign shrines:

> *And specially from every shires ende*
> *Of Engelond to Caunterbury they wende,*
> *The hooly blisful martir for to seke*
> *That hem hath holpen whan that*
> *they were seeke.*

('And, in England especially, they make their way from the corners of every county to Canterbury to seek out the blessed martyr who has helped them when they were sick'.) The 'hooly blisful martir' who could intercede for them is Archbishop Thomas Becket, murdered at the altar of his Cathedral by agents of King Henry II in 1170. He was immediately venerated as a saint, and his shrine became the centre of a major European cult.

BELOW: *Outrage at Becket's murder spread his cult through Europe. Relics were sought after. Many reliquaries survive, most in Limoges enamel, such as this fine example, c.1180. This* chasse *shows Henry's knights attacking Thomas at the altar; above is the deathbed scene.*

OPPOSITE: *Martyrdom of Becket from a Book of Hours, produced in the southern Netherlands during the fifteenth century. The Archbishop is shown kneeling at an altar in his Cathedral. Reginald Fitzurse raises a sword, another knight a poignard. Below are prayers to the Saint, beginning with decorated initial 'G'.*

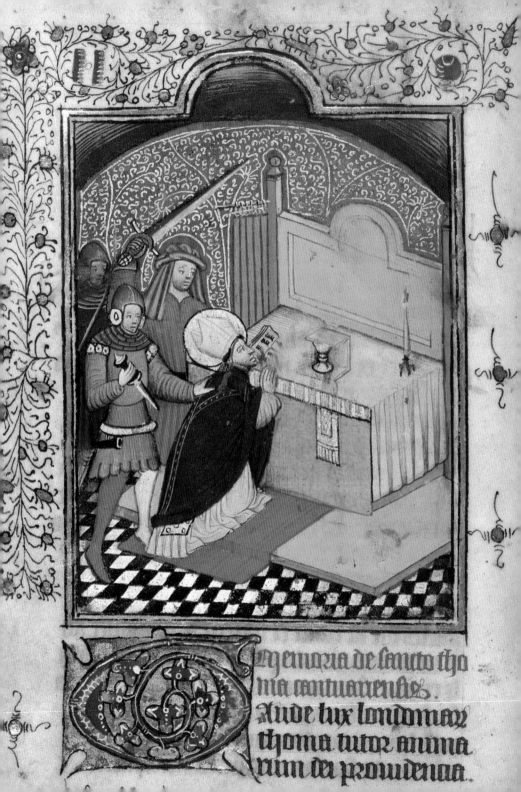

Memoria de sancto tho
ma cantuariensis.

Aude tux londomar
thoma tutor anima
rum dei prouidencia.

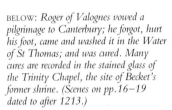

BELOW: *Roger of Valognes vowed a pilgrimage to Canterbury; he forgot, hurt his foot, came and washed it in the Water of St Thomas; and was cured. Many cures are recorded in the stained glass of the Trinity Chapel, the site of Becket's former shrine. (Scenes on pp.16–19 dated to after 1213.)*

RIGHT: *Walter of Lisors rides out of the city of Canterbury. His arms and face suggest that he is offering gratitude to God for having been cured.*

✠ DETVM ET IN VOTO LAVACRO·
PRECE SANGVINE POTO·

BELOW: *Godwin of Boxgrove, a leper, had a vision of Thomas giving away clothes. Finding himself cured, Godwin gave his shirt to the monks as a thank-offering to the Saint. The cures are shown in the ambulatory around the site of the shrine.*

LEFT: *Henry of Fordwich,
cured of his madness, gives
(below) the sticks and ropes
used to restrain him as a
thank-offering.*

OPPOSITE: *Matilda of Cologne
went mad after she heard that
her brother had killed the man
she loved. She lashed out and
killed her infant child, presumably
her child by this lover. Forcibly
brought to Canterbury, beaten
into submission and left bound
in front of the tomb, she calmed.
In a vision, Thomas told her to
go on pilgrimage to Compostella.*

RIGHT: *Saved from a fever as a
child by the Water of St Thomas,
Geoffrey of Winchester is again
saved by the intercession of
Thomas. His mother leans
over the boy, found among the
ruins of their collapsed house.*

Canterbury Cathedral

The Cathedral that we see today was begun in 1067 after a fire at the old cathedral, itself a successor to the church that was the see of St Augustine, the first Archbishop of Canterbury in 597. Pope Gregory the Great had sent Augustine and forty other monks from his own monastery in Rome to convert the pagan Angles. Augustine's *cathedra* (Greek: chair, throne, seat, see) symbolised his apostolic authority, conferred by the Pope and inherited by his successors. St Thomas's shrine grew very rich, as did Canterbury, a monastic Cathedral. In 1533 the Pope accepted Henry VIII's nomination of Thomas Cranmer for the see of Canterbury, which had fallen vacant. Cranmer supported Henry's plan to annul his twenty-four-year marriage with Catherine of Aragon so that he could marry Anne Boleyn, his mistress. So it was that the Church in England became the Church of England, and its Supreme Head was now not the successor to St Peter but the King himself. Henry wished to destroy the memory of a martyr who had died in defence of the rights of the Church against those of the Crown. The gold and jewels were stripped from Thomas's shrine and taken to London in twenty-one carts, an operation which took ten days. Canterbury's monks also lost their land to the Crown.

Canterbury Cathedral floodlit at night, from the south-west. Had they reached Canterbury, Chaucer's pilgrims would first have seen the Cathedral from the north side.

The Pilgrimage Route

The *Tales* are told by pilgrims riding from London along the Roman road known as Watling Street and through the countryside of Kent to Canterbury. The ride took two days, usually with a night at Rochester. Geoffrey Chaucer himself, who lived in Kent and represented the county in Parliament, will surely have ridden to Canterbury, both on business and as a pilgrim. The *Tales* mention places on the road: the pilgrims water their horses at the second milestone from London on the Old Kent Road, at a ford known as 'the watering place of St Thomas'. The road follows the Thames. The Host points out Deptford, and then cries out: 'Lo Greenwich, where many a shrew is inne.' A 'shrew' was a villain or criminal; Chaucer himself lived in Greenwich from 1385 to 1399. He often makes such jokes against himself. Other places are mentioned as the *Tales* go on, the last of which are Boghton under Blee, and Bobbe-up-and-Down, little places very near to Canterbury. Watling Street was also the route to Dover and, from there, to France, Flanders (the birthplace of Chaucer's wife) and Italy.

The high altar in the quire of the Cathedral. Above and behind, eastern light from the Trinity Chapel, where stood the shrine of St Thomas, destroyed in 1539 by agents of Henry VIII. After the fire of 1174, the architects of the new quire and Chapel were William of Sens and his successor, William the Englishman.

Chaucer's Life

Geoffrey had been born in the Vintry, the wine-merchants' street, in London, still a walled city; its population was about 30,000. The Chaucers had come from Ipswich to London, there acquiring a French-derived name (*chausseur*, *chaussier*: shoemaker, hosier). Geoffrey's grandfather and John Chaucer, his father, were wine merchants in London. John was a butler (*bouteiller*) at court; he married Agnes Copton, who inherited the estate of Hamo de Copton, the moneyer of the Tower of London. Their son Geoffrey became a royal servant, a 'King's man'. Geoffrey's son Thomas was to become the King's own butler, and a wealthy man, five times Speaker of the House of Commons. Alice, Thomas's daughter, married first the Earl of Salisbury, and then the Duke of Suffolk. Life was short, and marriages shorter; Chaucer's own mother married three times, as did his father's mother. One of his pilgrims, the Wife of Bath, advertises herself as looking for a sixth husband; she goes on a lot of pilgrimages.

Chaucer's background was mercantile, but his career was that of a 'King's man', doing the things administrators and diplomats do in the modern civil service. He grew up attached to courts, and his audience included courtiers, but his official duties brought him into contact with a range of people, and his associates included London merchants and some learned Oxford men. His career began as a page in the household of the Countess of Ulster, wife to Edward III's second surviving son, Lionel, Duke of Clarence.

LEFT: *A view westwards over the Tower of London to London Bridge, from a manuscript of the poems of Charles d'Orléans, c.1500. Chaucer was born among the buildings shown on the north bank, in the Vintry. The French poet, captured at Agincourt in 1415, and a prisoner in England for twenty-two years, is seen writing, then standing at a window, then dispatching a letter in the courtyard.*

PAGE 26: *Miniature from* Grandes Chroniques de France, *c.1415, by the Workshop of the Boucicaut Master, depicting Anglo-French chivalric warfare: a battle between Louis IX of France and Henry III of England. When, a century later, Chaucer went to fight in France, Edward III put the lilies of France into the English arms (see p.27).*

In his teens Chaucer fought in John of Gaunt's expedition to France and was captured. In 1360 Edward III paid a ransom of £16 towards his release. He was sent on a diplomatic mission to Spain in 1366, which was also the year of his marriage to Philippa from Hainault, in French-speaking Flanders. (He thus followed the example of Edward III, who, in 1328, the second year of his reign, had married a Philippa of Hainault.) Philippa Chaucer bore a son, Thomas, in 1367. On the death of Prince Lionel in 1368, Chaucer entered the service of John of Gaunt, Duke of Lancaster, the third son of Edward III. Gaunt, the greatest subject in the land, later became a counsellor to his nephew, King Richard II. Later still, John of Gaunt married as his third wife Katherine Swynford, Philippa Chaucer's sister. Katherine had been Gaunt's mistress before his second marriage to Blanche of Castile. In 1369 Chaucer was again with Gaunt in Picardy, and from 1370 until 1373 he went on government

EDVARDI TERTI
CASTELLÆ ET
DVX LANCAS
CONSTABVLAR
DE QVEENSBOV
TO OCTOBRIS
REGNI ELOVTE
GIÆ 50 FRA

QVI
MAL Y PENSE
HONI SOIT

missions to Genoa and Florence. In 1374 he was appointed Controller of the Customs and Subsidy of Wools, Skins and Hides, England's chief trade. In 1376 he was paid for some unspecified secret service. In 1377 he went on a secret mission to Flanders, and then to France to negotiate peace with Charles V. In 1378 he was on a diplomatic mission to the Lord of Milan. In the 1380s he lived in London and held an important office in the customs of the port of London. In the year in which the *Tales* begin, 1387, Chaucer was Member of Parliament for Kent, and a Justice of the Peace. It was in 1387 also that his wife Philippa died. In 1390 Chaucer, at that time Clerk for the King's Works, was robbed and beaten; he retired from public life. From then on he was writing his *Tales*.

Chaucer the Poet

Chaucer is the first English poet to have been read in every generation since his death. He wrote exclusively in English, and was the first major European poet to do so. His friend John Gower, a poet ten years older than he, wrote in English, French and Latin. Learned Europeans spoke Latin; French was the fashion in courts throughout Europe, and the language of the English court had long been French. Parliament was held in English for the first time in 1363, and Henry V (1413–22) liked to speak English rather than French. Chaucer began his writing career by translating *Le Roman de la Rose* and imitating French poets. But on his second Italian visit, to the Visconti Lord of Milan, he began to read the Tuscan poems of Boccaccio, Petrarch and Dante. His great poem *Troilus and Criseyde* (1385) has many deliberate echoes of Dante. The *Tales* include many set in Europe, but the telling of the tales is set in Kent, and their tellers are recognisably English.

Chaucer's Englishness is unmistakable, not least in his social sense of humour. We have seen that he was a customs officer, a trusted royal servant, a seasoned diplomat. In his writings, however, he presents himself as easily abashed and slightly foolish. Chaucer puts himself into most of his longer poems. His early works present him as bookish, bemused or at a loss. In the *Tales* he is invited to tell a tale by the Host of the Tabard, who makes jokes about Chaucer's portly figure, his 'elvish' countenance, and his retreating manner. Chaucer's first tale is a remarkably silly story, with a comically inept use of language, about a knight called Sir Topaz. It is a sophisticated

LEFT: *The finest portrait of Geoffrey Chaucer, his face grave and sensitive. It was commissioned by Thomas Hoccleve, who revered Chaucer as his poetic master. The poet points to the stanza of Hoccleve's* The Regimen of Princes *in which Hoccleve explains his purpose: to show exactly what Chaucer looked like so that others will remember him.*

PAGES 32-3: *The Prioress is shown riding side-saddle, the more elegant way of riding for ladies introduced by Queen Anne. She raises one hand in greeting. The other, holding the bridle, has a rosary round the wrist. The wimple exposes the forehead, as was fashionable. The miniature faces the beginning of her (anti-Semitic) legend of little William of Norwich.*

parody of the unsophisticated rhyming romances that were then popular in England. The Host, the referee of the tale-telling game, does not realise this and stops Chaucer short, hotly informing his creator that his rhyming 'is not worth a turd'. Chaucer retaliates mildly by telling a moral tale in prose: a lengthy moral allegory showing how an angry husband can be tamed by a virtuous wife. (The bullying Host much later confesses that he is a hen-pecked husband.) Chaucer also presents himself as overawed or impressed by everyone he meets, except for manifest villains of the lowest class. Chaucer was a good observer and a better listener. Dialogue between the pilgrims, or between the characters in their stories, provides the liveliest language in the *Canterbury Tales*.

An ability to be interested and to seem impressed must have helped Chaucer in his professional life. Thomas Hoccleve, a younger poet who knew and admired Chaucer, wrote of him that 'he seyde alwey the beste'. The way Chaucer introduces the pilgrims in the Prologue shows that he has the diplomat's gift of inviting confidences, getting people to talk – and to give themselves away. Although Chaucer had learned friends who would have read his poems silently to themselves, his works would normally have been read aloud, initially by the poet himself. So Chaucer's apparent naivety is an aspect of his personality which he heightens in his work – a game which is part of his English sense of humour.

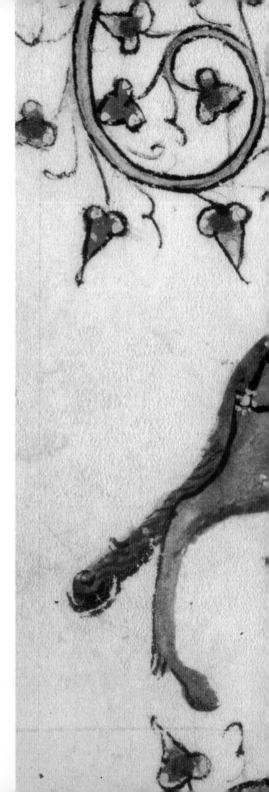

The Pilgrims

Chaucer's subject matter in some of the *Canterbury Tales*, his last work, is also English. Most of the Prologue to the *Tales* is taken up with vivid portraits of his fellow pilgrims, who represent an almost complete cross-section of society; only those at the very top and the very bottom of the feudal pyramid are lacking: no nobles, no serfs. Only a few women are included; women were normally not free to travel. Chaucer's Knight, Squire and Yeoman represent the military estate in medieval society. His Prioress, Monk and Friar represent the religious estate. The third estate, that of the workers, is largest, since it includes all non-military lay people: Merchant, Clerk of Oxford (a logician), Man of Law, Franklin (a country squire), Shipman, Doctor, Wife of Bath. These portraits, and Chaucer's ideal Parson and Ploughman, give us memorable ideas of medieval English people, ideas we still retain. Most of these types have recognisable modern descendants, as do the pompous Guildsmen and their villainous Cook, and also the thieving Reeve (estate manager), Manciple (college bursar) and Miller. Bringing up the rear are the Pardoner and the Summoner, clerical parasites with no direct modern descendants, and, last of all, Chaucer himself. Most of the thirty pilgrims tell a tale, and Chaucer tells two, neither of which would have won him a free dinner. Each pilgrim was supposed to tell more than one tale, and the work is far from complete, but Chaucer did provide an ending. When Canterbury is in sight the Parson gives what is offered as the final tale,

a treatise on penance, in order to remind us that life is a pilgrimage – to a heavenly city. The twenty-three preceding tales are very various and include saints' lives, romances, tragedies and moralities; they also show plenty of comical immorality and vulgarity. The 'low' stories told by the churls predominate in stage adaptations of the *Canterbury Tales*. This gives the impression that Chaucer chiefly wrote bawdy stories, but reflects modern tastes. Funny as they are, the churls' tales form only a minor part of the *Canterbury Tales,* which are of various kinds and, taken as a whole, offer a decidedly Christian kind of comedy.

OPPOSITE: *The Wife of Bath is the reverse of the Prioress. A survivor of three rich old husbands and two young ones, she is looking for a sixth. The widow rides astride, with sharp spurs and a whip – for men as well as for horses.*

PAGE 36: *The Kelmscott Chaucer, designed and printed by William Morris at the Kelmscott Press, 1896, illustrated by Edward Burne-Jones. Chaucer is shown palely composing in a garden by a well. The opening of the Prologue, 'Whan that Aprille …', is designed to look like a medieval manuscript.*

PAGE 37: *Portrait of Henry IV by an unknown artist, sixteenth or early seventeenth century. At the death of his father, John of Gaunt, Henry Bolingbroke was disinherited by Richard II in 1399. He deposed Richard and ruled until 1413: the first Lancastrian King of England.*

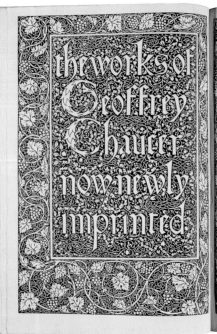

Last Years

After Richard's forced abdication, the
new King, Henry IV, John of Gaunt's son,
confirmed Chaucer in his royal pensions
and in his office of substitute forester
of the royal forest of North Petherton in
Somerset. In 1400 Chaucer took a lease
on a house in the garden of the Lady
Chapel of Westminster Abbey, to the
west of the city of London, but he died
on 25 October 1400. He was buried in
the Abbey, founded at Westminster by
King Edward the Confessor in 1065. Most
English monarchs have been crowned in
Westminster Abbey by an Archbishop
of Canterbury, and some have been
buried there. In 1400 Westminster, like
Canterbury, was a Benedictine abbey.
Edmund Spenser (d. 1599) was the
first of many poets to be buried near

Chaucer, whose grave had been moved
in 1556 to a part of the south transept
since called Poets' Corner. Although
English poetry goes back to Anglo-
Saxon times, and although there were
fine poets in Chaucer's day, such as
John Gower, William Langland and the
anonymous author of *Sir Gawain and
the Green Knight*, Chaucer's reputation
was greater. He was looked up to by
his successors, and his works, printed
by Caxton, are the only verse literature
from the Middle Ages to have remained
continuously in print since Caxton. He
was imitated by Spenser, Shakespeare
and other poets, and John Dryden
(d. 1700) called him the Father of
English Poetry.

HENRICVS IIII

ABOVE:
John Lydgate, a
Benedictine monk, wrote
a continuation of the
Canterbury Tales.
This miniature, showing
Lydgate in the centre of a
group of pilgrims leaving
Canterbury, is from the
Prologue to Lydgate's
The Siege of Thebes.

FRONT COVER:
Geoffrey Chaucer,
artist and date unknown.
A version of the traditional
portrait showing the Father
of English Poetry: gravely
bearded, patriarchal.
His 'penner' or pen-case
indicates that he is a
writer; in the other
hand, a rosary.

INSIDE COVERS:
William Blake's vision
of the pilgrimage leaving
Southwark, tempera
on canvas, c.1809.
Prominent are, left to
right: Chaucer (red),
Miller (with bagpipes),
Wife of Bath (red
stockings), Parson
(black); then (rear)
Host, Pardoner,
Prioress, Knight.

REAR COVER:
Pilgrims on the road to
Canterbury, a modern
re-creation from the
Trinity Chapel at
Canterbury Cathedral.

© Scala Publishers Ltd, 2012
Text © Michael Alexander, 2012
Photography © Cathedral Enterprises Ltd
(pp.22–3 by Robert Greshoff / ArcEye
Images), except for: front cover © Dean and
Chapter of Westminster; inside cover
© Culture and Sport Glasgow (Museums) / The
Bridgeman Art Library; p.2 © the Huntington
Library, San Marino, California, ms. EL 26 C 9
('The Ellesmere Chaucer') EL 26 c9 f153v; p.4
© the Huntington Library, San Marino,
California, ms. EL 26 C 9 ('The Ellesmere
Chaucer') EL 26 c9 f115v; p.5 © the Master
and Fellows of Corpus Christi College,
Cambridge; p.6 © National Portrait Gallery,
London; p.7 © The British Library Board
Royal 6 E. VI, f.301; p.8 © British Library
Board. All Rights Reserved / The Bridgeman
Art Library; p.9 © Dean and Chapter of
Westminster; pp.10–11 © The British Library
Board Royal 18 E. I f.165v; pp.12–13 © Neil
Holmes / The Bridgeman Art Library; p.14
© Victoria and Albert Museum, London; p.15
© The British Library Board Harley 2982,
f.13v; p.24 © The British Library Board Royal
16 F. II f.73; pp.26 © The British Library
Board Cotton Nero E. II pt.2, f.40v; p.27
© Private Collection / The Bridgeman Art
Library; p.28 © Dean and Chapter of
Westminster; p.29 © British Library Board.
All Rights Reserved / The Bridgeman Art
Library; pp.30–1 © The British Library Board
Harley 4866, f.88; pp.32–3 © the Huntington
Library, San Marino, California, ms. EL 26 C 9
('The Ellesmere Chaucer') EL 26 c9 f148v;
p.34 © the Huntington Library, San Marino,
California, ms. EL 26 C 9 ('The Ellesmere
Chaucer') EL 26 c9 f72; p.36 © Cheltenham
Art Gallery & Museums, Gloucestershire, UK /
The Bridgeman Art Library; p.37 © National
Portrait Gallery, London; and p.38–9 © The
British Library Board Royal 18 D. II f.148

First published in 2012 by
Scala Publishers Ltd
Northburgh House
10 Northburgh St
London EC1V 0AT
Telephone: +44 (0) 20 7490 9900
www.scalapublishers.com

in association with
Cathedral Enterprises Ltd
25 Burgate
Canterbury
Kent CT1 2HA
Telephone: +44 (0) 1227 865 300
www.cathedral-enterprises.co.uk

ISBN: 978 1 85759 748 6

Editor: Esme West

Design: Trevor Wilson Design Ltd

Printed and bound in Turkey

10 9 8 7 6 5 4 3 2 1

British Library Cataloguing in
Publication Data

A catalogue record for this book is
available from the British Library.